PINA
BAUSCH

Swimming with Elephants
P U B L I C A T I O N S

Thanks to Editions du Cygne, Paris for the original publication in 2013

Cover Art Copyright © 2018 Jami Proctor-Xu

ISBN-13:
978-0999892930

PINA BAUSCH

by
Werner Lambersy

Translated from French
by
Jack Hirschman

Introduction to Werner Lambersy

One wonders why this is virtually the first book of Werner Lambersy's published in the U.S. The poet has not only published more than 40 books in French but the range and depth of his work is very striking. Perhaps it's because he is not French by birth but was born in Anvers, Belgium, in 1941 and settled in Paris in 1980, where the major body of his works has been written over the past 35 years. His insistence on the unreligious if not irreligious aspect of mysticism, especially with respect to the poetic word itself, is a central point of his philosophy of the word, and any deep reading of his poetry will reveal a poet very much in command of his lines and of the feelings he is intending to evoke.

He takes his books "as they come," so to speak, meaning that he allows them to unfold their forms as *they* and not *he* wishes. Perhaps that is why this book, an exquisite homage to one of the most extraordinary modern dancers since WWII, Pina Bausch, fundamentally attempts to reveal her, in gesture, motions, dance positions, through as it were an haiku-like prismatic: the whole book is

composed---with few exceptions---of brief,
epiphanic three-line insights into Pina Bausch.

Lambersy doesn't count syllables; he's not
writing haikus but he clearly has recognized a
relationship between such brilliant brevities as the
haiku evokes regarding time and space, and the
gestures of perhaps Germany's most wonderful
dancer of the past generation: Bausch was born in
1940 at the start of the war, in Nazi Germany, and
died in Germany in 2009, after having attained
world-wide renown, including years with the
Metropolitan Opera Ballet Company and Paul
Taylor's New American Ballet in New York, a city
she described as a "jungle" but one where "you
have the feeling of total freedom" and where, she
believed, she had discovered the essence of herself
as a dancer.

I believe there may very well be a deeper
synchronicity with respect to this book, which was
published in Paris by Editions du Cygne in 2013,---
four years after her death---, and Pina Bausch
herself. Lambersy was born in 1941, that is only a
year after Pina Bausch. His life has been haunted
by the fact that his father left him and his family in
Belgium to fight with the German Army as a Nazi.

Werner has written about his father and his own torment growing up, in some excellent poems in other books of his. Pina Bausch, who was raised in East Germany during the Cold War years, methinks represents in Werner's book an artistic transfiguration of his youthful agonies, which have pursued him all his life. That is, I think this book is more than an artistic appreciation, more even than an "exquisite homage." It is the triumph of Art itself through the Beauty that,

> "drop by drop
>
>> will pierce the toughest
>> steel of the soul"

as Dance, as this Tanztheater (which Bausch is known for having invented) of haikuesque "drops" are here presented by Lambersy as the tears of a generation visited by some of the most horrible monstrosities that the human soul has ever had to engage.

I met Werner Lambersy for the first time in Paris one June some years ago, at La Marche de la Poesie, the celebration of small poetry presses in France, as my books are published there by Le

Temps des Cerises. I recall us speaking briefly at that time. But it was through Ferruccio Brugnaro, the grand Italian poet whom I've translated and published in the United States and who since become a friend of Werner's, that Lambersy has sent me some of his books, one of which is this one.

I'd like to thank Jami Proctor-Xu, poet and translator from Chinese who, when I mentioned the name Pina Bausch, expressed her deep love for Pina's work. She has provided the cover art for this engagement with the work of Werner Lambersy in the United States.

Jack Hirschman
San Francisco, 2018

"Dance, dance, otherwise we're lost"

~Pina Bausch

Pina Bausch, 1966
Photography by Walter Vogel

Pina Bausch
Dances with her eyes
She looks out

Even with eyes closed
She sees

You feel the light favor
Of her regard

You know it's there
The dance
Begins

You understand:
Blue isn't a
Cold color

Which burns
Without burning or ash

The sea's
Just sea under
The wave

The rest
Sounds of spume
Over the drowned gestures

The sky and the sea
The same color

The horizon
Never has a frontier

Anymore than death
Separates the soul and
The body

Soul and flesh
Dance under one of a kind
Eyelid

Pina Bausch
Begins where she withdraws
Her gaze

You realize
She wants to be united
With the universal

Blindness
In order to begin
Where Sensitivity feels its way

Like the fleeting
Weightless and disconnected
Dance

Indifferent
Next to the wind
That carries her longing

But never to the bright
Light where she'll
Die

Like the eagle facing
When the sun
Blinds

Pina Bausch
Dances to begin with with
Palm

A mute map
With lines to the wide-open sky

The elegant swan's neck
Of her wrist
Palm up

The reed of a gesture
On the shadow curve
Of the horizon

With her fingers
The length of wild
Amianthus

The Aurora Borealis
Looking for
Solar eruptions

And the shooting star
Of loving disorder

With shadows
Of the catalpa tree like her
Large hand-span

The long
White palm of her arm
Brought down

Onto her naked bony
Birdy snowy
Breast

On the petals
Of a breath provided
With magnolias

May the pale mist
Sweep away the breath
Under the weight

Of the dew of the silence

And the charge
Of beauties you can't
Hold back

Pina Bausch dances with
Head and shoulder

Heading
Entrance of the church
Keystone of the arches

The chorus
Where she involves both us
And her troupe

Café Muller
Where the chairs of the world
Are topsy-turvy

For who is she
Who moves so on the side
Of the void

For who is she
Who undresses the loneliness
Of longing

For who is she
Who dances what we
Husband

And the wife
Being more fragile who
Runs away

And comes back
And trembles becoming crazy
And knowing everything

Because touching already
Belongs to love
And dancing

An exorcism
And a bewitchment
In order not to be dissolved

Disappearing
After the apocalypse
Of the chaste drawing near

This last sun will perish
Say the Inca
Gomara then Montaigne

Levi-Strauss:
You've passed the point of
No return

Sixth destruction
Of the blue world but not
Of life

Pina Bausch
Dances the divine panic
Of the body

Like a temple
When the rock that founds
It trembles

Like a couple
Under the dying orgasm
Of the thunderbolt

Pina Bausch
Dances with hipbones
Of flesh which move

Tie themselves together
Turn over reappear
Showing the back of the cards

Under the mark
Forbidden depth of
Schools of fish

Of longing
And the unedited monsters
Of loneliness

In the bitter resemblance
To great depths
Of dead coral

With space for extinguished
Stars

Pina Bausch
Can dance a tableau

So the cornices
Of beauty are held
Hooked up to the sky

So it's true
One doesn't know where
To put all the movement

Her feet
Flinging her body
Into space

Confronting the walls
That hem the air in

To the burden which weighs on
The surfaces of
The skin

In the time that uses itself
As long as it lasts

Pina Bausch
Can dance motionless
And show how

She who dances
And constitutes the substance
Of the Russian dolls of
The universe

Her stride is contained
In her fall

And the bonds
The leaps of the little kid
Of Desire

Which can't
Remain so without
Falling back

Into the violent order

Into the position
Where Pina Bausch waits for
The passage

Of the comets of love

The obstinate drop by drop
Of beauty

Which will go through
The toughest steel of the soul